Mel Bay Presents

Fingerpicking Guitar
for the Young Beginner

By
William
Bay

CD CONTENTS

1. Tune-Up [2:02]
2. Brother John [:28]
3. Brother John-Plucking Style [:28]
4. Farmer in the Dell-Thumb Strum Version [:19]
5. Farmer in the Dell-Plucking Version [:18]
6. Brother John-Arpeggio Style [:27]
7. Farmer in the Dell-Arpeggio Style [:17]
8. Father Abraham-Thumb Strum [:26]
9. Father Abraham-Plucking Version [:27]
10. Father Abraham-Arpeggio Style [:28]
11. Father Abraham-Double Arpeggio Pattern [:29]
12. Lonesome Valley-Strum Style [:41]
13. Lonesome Valley-Arpeggio Style [:41]
14. Lonesome Valley-Double Arpeggio Pattern [:51]
15. Lonesome Valley-Alternate Bass [:50]
16. Tom Dooley-Double Arpeggio Pattern [:28]
17. Tom Dooley-Alternate Bass Pattern [:28]
18. Old Chisholm Trail-Double Arpeggio Pattern [:28]
19. Old Chisholm Trail-Alternate Bass Pattern [:29]
20. Skip to my Lou-Alternate Bass [:27]
21. Long Long Ago-Alternate Bass [:28]
22. Down in the Valley-3/4 Strum [:28]
23. Down in the Valley-3/4 Arpeggio Pattern [:30]
24. Oh, My Darling Clementine-3/4 Arpeggio Pattern [:24]
25. Oh, Mary, Don't You Weep-Strum Style [:47]
26. Blow Ye Winds, Westerly-3/4 Strum [:33]
27. Our Team Will Shine Tonight [:46]
28. Jack of Diamonds [:22]
29. She'll Be Coming 'Round the Mountain-Alternate Bass Pattern [:44]
30. Hey Lolly-Double Arpeggio [:25]
31. Pay Me My Money Down-Double Arpeggio [:26]
32. On Top of Old Smokey-3/4 Arpeggio [1:04]
33. Auld Lang Syne-Alternate Bass [:53]
34. Streets of Laredo [:41]
35. Beautiful Brown Eyes-Bass-Pluck-Pluck Pattern [:36]
36. Hey, Ho, Nobody Home-Arpeggio Pattern [:27]
37. Shady Grove-Alternate Bass [:29]
38. Oh, Sinner Man-Alternate Bass [:27]

1 2 3 4 5 6 7 8 9 0

Visit us on the Web at www.melbay.com — E-mail us at email@melbay.com

How to Select a Guitar

When selecting a guitar for a child, it is essential that the instrument obtained is not too big for the student. For most children, I recommend a student-size or a 3/4 size guitar. In addition, you must make certain that the neck is not too wide. Be sure to take the student in and let the student hold the instrument to see if it is manageable. Also, check the strings to make certain that they are not too high off the fingerboard at the nut or first fret (consult the parts of the guitar diagram to see where this is). Also, your teacher may help you check whether or not there are string buzzes or some other problem with the instrument. Most of the student-model guitars being made today are of a very good quality and many of the problems which used to plague beginning guitarists are no longer concerns.

The Guitar and its Parts

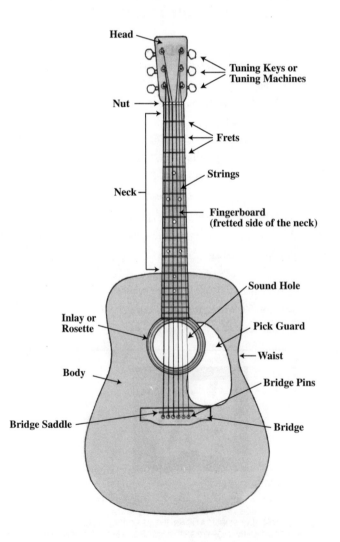

Holding the Guitar

Position the guitar so that you are comfortable. The right hand should rest over the sound hole. The left hand should be able to reach the first fret.

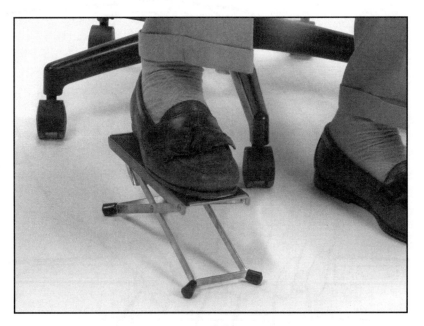

A footstool can be purchased at your local music store. The footstool is adjustable and can help elevate the guitar to a comfortable height.

Right Hand Position

The right arm should pivot approximately at the widest point on the instrument. Make certain that the elbow and wrist are loose. The right arm should feel comfortable to you. The tone will vary depending upon where the strings are plucked. The closer that we play to the fingerboard, the more mellow the tone. The sound is correspondingly sharper as we play closer to the bridge. The fingers should be held loosely so that flexibility can be attained. Make certain that your wrist and fingers are not held in a rigid, stiff manner.

Right Hand Fingers Touching String

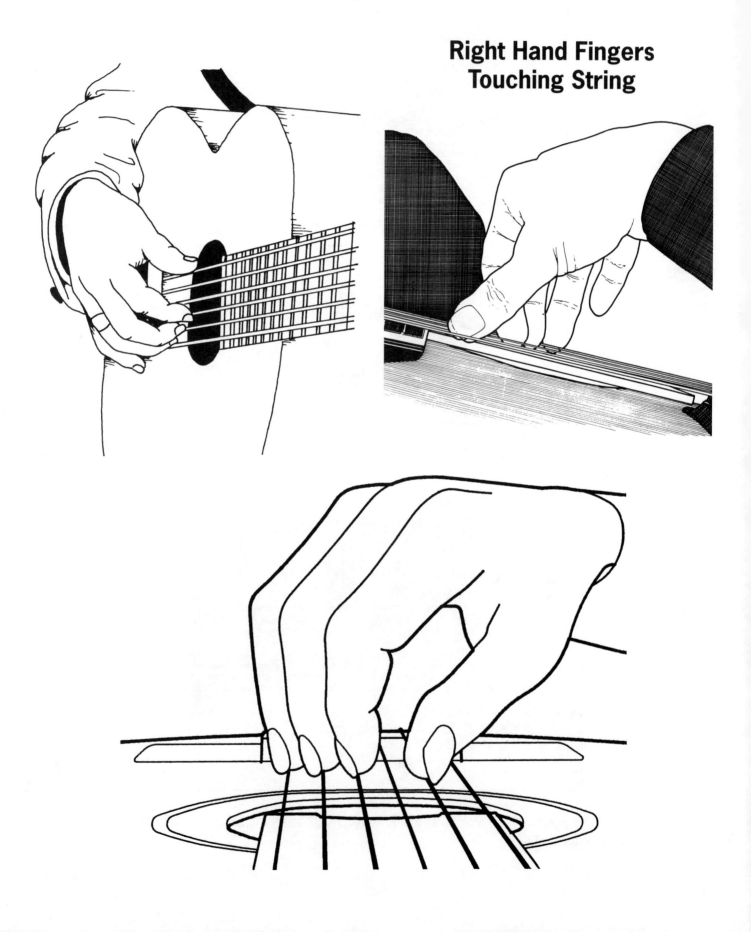

Left Hand Positioning

To begin with, keep the left elbow and wrist relaxed. Avoid positioning that strains and tightens your left wrist and elbow. The important thing to remember is to place the left hand so that the hand is arched and so that the fingers can fall straight down on the strings. Greater technique can he obtained by pressing down on the strings with the tips of the fingers than with the fleshy part. Also. it is important to bring the fingers directly down on the strings so that part of the finger does not accidentally touch and muffle one of the other strings.

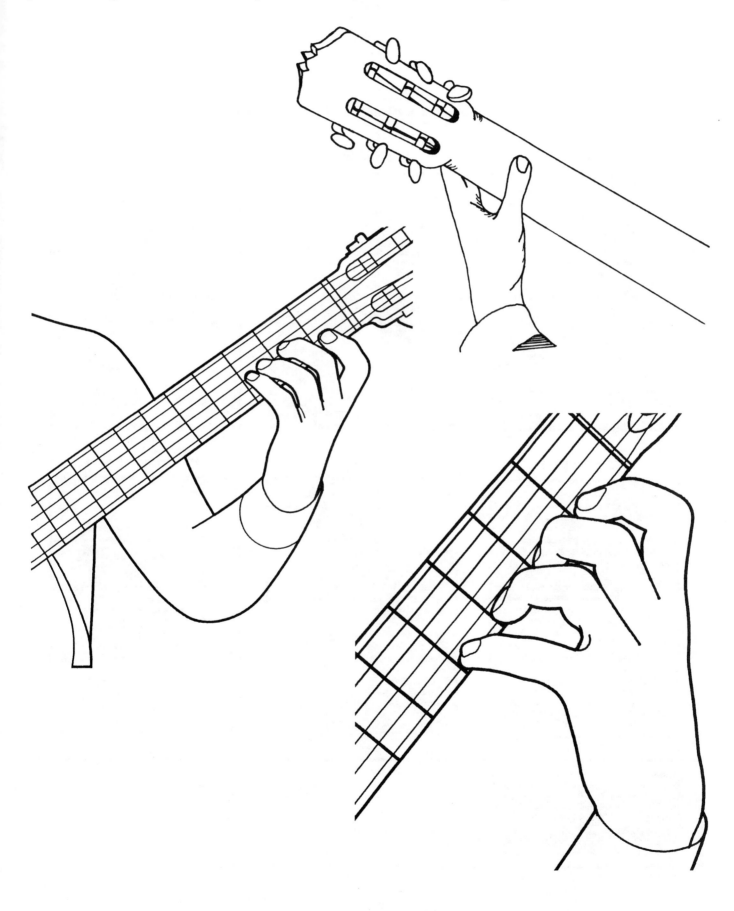

Tuning the Guitar

6th 5th 4th 3rd 2nd 1st

Listen to track #1 of your CD and tune up as follows!

1st String – E

2nd String – B

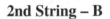

3rd String – G

4th String – D

5th String – A

6th String – Low E

Electronic Guitar Tuner

Electronic Guitar Tuners are available at your music store. They are a handy device and highly recommended.

Left Hand Fingering   Right Hand Fingering

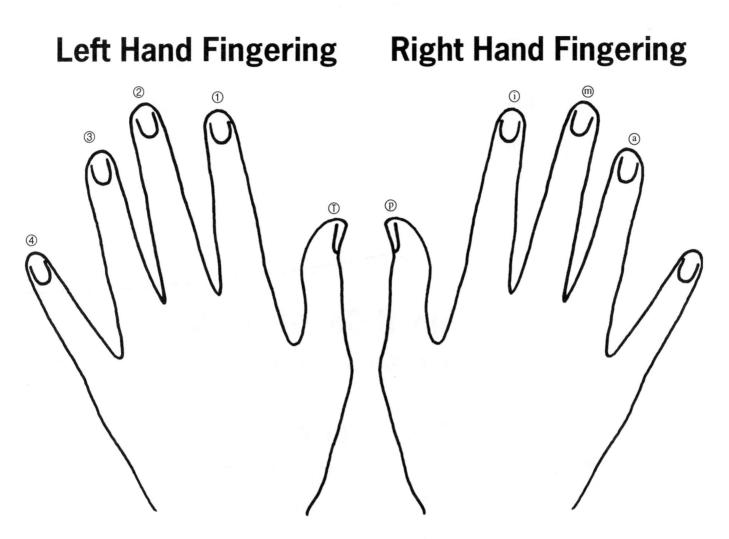

Right-hand finger symbols are derived from Spanish. The letters stand for:

Symbol	Spanish	English
p	Pulgar	Thumb
i	Índice	Index Finger
m	Medio	Middle Finger
a	Anular	Ring Finger

Counting

We will use the following **Time Signatures**.

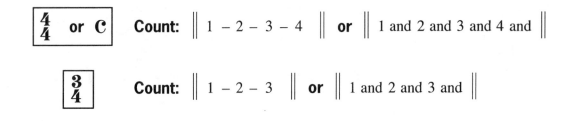

$\frac{4}{4}$ or **C**   **Count:** ‖ 1 – 2 – 3 – 4 ‖ **or** ‖ 1 and 2 and 3 and 4 and ‖

$\frac{3}{4}$ **Count:** ‖ 1 – 2 – 3 ‖ **or** ‖ 1 and 2 and 3 and ‖

Explanation of Chord Symbols

[Our First Chord – G/EZ Form]

G/EZ Form

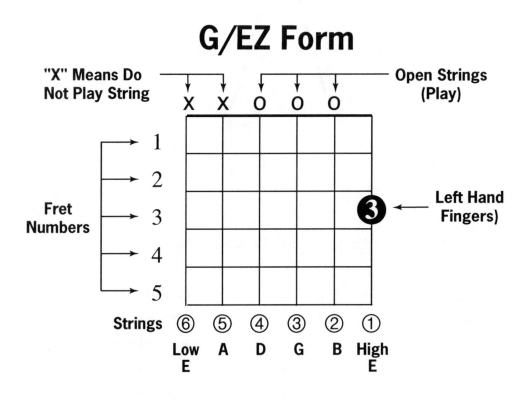

Strumming
Symbol

Down Strum

↓

**Strum down towards floor
using your thumb**

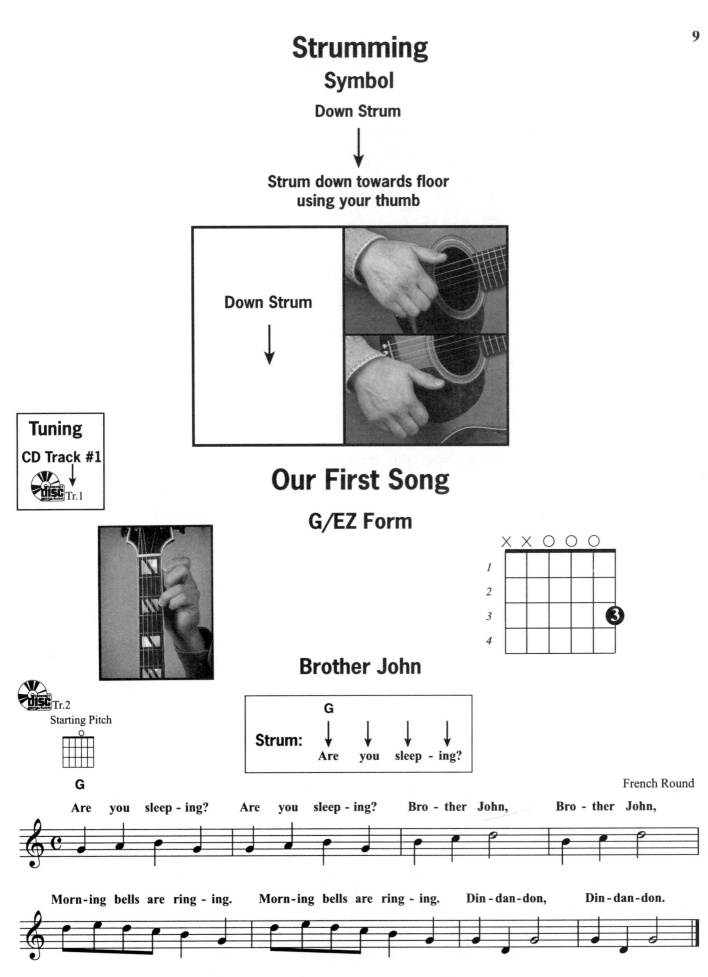

Down Strum

↓

Tuning

CD Track #1

Tr.1

Our First Song
G/EZ Form

X X O O O

1
2
3 ❸
4

Brother John

Tr.2
Starting Pitch

G

Strum: G ↓ ↓ ↓ ↓
Are you sleep - ing?

G

French Round

Are you sleep - ing? Are you sleep - ing? Bro - ther John, Bro - ther John,

Morn-ing bells are ring - ing. Morn-ing bells are ring - ing. Din - dan - don, Din - dan - don.

French: Frè-re Jac-ques, Frè-re Jac-ques, Dor-mez vous? Dor-mez vous?
Son-nez les matines, Son-nez les matines, Di, din, don! Di, din, don!

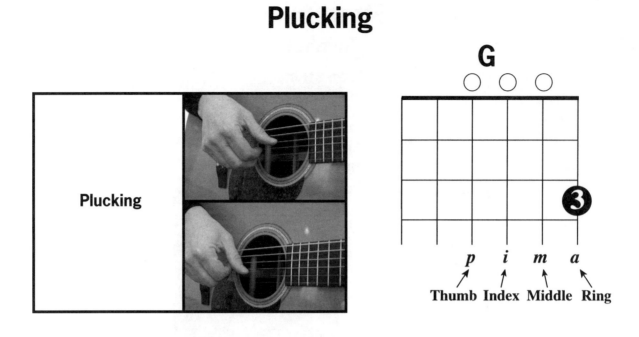

Plucking

Place your right hand fingers on the strings as shown above. While your left hand fingers the EZ G chord, pluck the top four strings by pulling your right-hand fingers off together.

Brother John Plucking Style

French: Frè-re Jac-ques, Frè-re Jac-ques, Dor-mez vous? Dor-mez vous?
Son-nez les matines, Son-nez les matines, Di, din, don! Di, din, don!

New Song
Farmer in the Dell
Thumb Strum Version

2. The farmer takes a wife
3. The wife takes a child
4. The child takes a nurse
5. The nurse takes a dog

6. The dog takes a cat.
7. The cat takes a rat.
8. The rat takes the cheese.
9. The cheese stands alone.

Farmer in the Dell
Plucking Version

2. The farmer takes a wife
3. The wife takes a child
4. The child takes a nurse
5. The nurse takes a dog

6. The dog takes a cat.
7. The cat takes a rat.
8. The rat takes the cheese.
9. The cheese stands alone.

Arpeggio Picking

With arpeggio picking we play one note at a time. Instead of plucking all notes together, play one note at a time.

Brother John
Arpeggio Style

Tr.6

Starting Pitch

G			
p	*i*	*m*	*a*
Are	you	sleep	- ing?

French Round

G

Are you sleep - ing? Are you sleep - ing? Bro - ther John, Bro - ther John,

Morn-ing bells are ring - ing. Morn-ing bells are ring - ing. Din - dan - don, Din - dan - don.

French: Frè-re Jac-ques, Frè-re Jac-ques, Dor-mez vous? Dor-mez vous?
           Son-nez les matines, Son-nez les matines, Di, din, don! Di, din, don!

Farmer in the Dell
Arpeggio Style

Tr.7

Starting Pitch

G			
p	*i*	*m*	*a*
The farmer	in the dell,		The

Folk Song

G

The far - mer in the dell, The far - mer in the dell,

Heigh, ho, the der - ry o! The far - mer in the dell!

2. The farmer takes a wife
3. The wife takes a child
4. The child takes a nurse
5. The nurse takes a dog

6. The dog takes a cat.
7. The cat takes a rat.
8. The rat takes the cheese.
9. The cheese stands alone.

D7 Chord

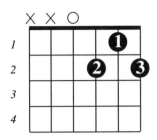

Strumming Different Chords

Practice

Father Abraham
Thumb Strum

Gospel Song

Father Ab - ra - ham had man - y kids, man - y

kids had Fa - ther Ab - ra - ham, I am one of them and so are

you, so let's all praise the Lord. 1. Right arm!

2. Right arm, Left arm.
3. Right arm, Left arm, Right foot.
4. Right arm, Left arm, Right foot, Left foot.
5. Right arm, Left arm, Right foot, Left foot, Turn around.
6. Right arm, Left arm, Right foot, Left foot, Turn around, Sit down!

Plucking the D7 Chord

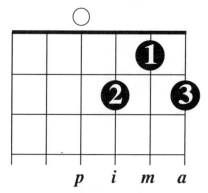

Plucking Different Chords

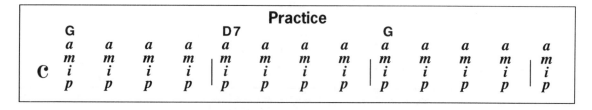

Father Abraham
Plucking Version

Gospel Song

2. Right arm, Left arm.

3. Right arm, Left arm, Right foot.

4. Right arm, Left arm, Right foot, Left foot.

5. Right arm, Left arm, Right foot, Left foot, Turn around.

6. Right arm, Left arm, Right foot, Left foot, Turn around, Sit down!

Arpeggio Picking Different Chords

Father Abraham
Arpeggio Style

2. Right arm, Left arm.
3. Right arm, Left arm, Right foot.
4. Right arm, Left arm, Right foot, Left foot.
5. Right arm, Left arm, Right foot, Left foot, Turn around.
6. Right arm, Left arm, Right foot, Left foot, Turn around, Sit down!

Doubling the Arpeggio Strum

We have been playing the arpeggio strum slowly.
Now we will play 2 patterns per measure.

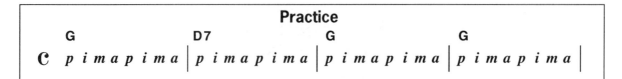

Father Abraham
Two Arpeggios per Measure

2. Right arm, Left arm.
3. Right arm, Left arm, Right foot.
4. Right arm, Left arm, Right foot, Left foot.
5. Right arm, Left arm, Right foot, Left foot, Turn around.
6. Right arm, Left arm, Right foot, Left foot, Turn around, Sit down!

Full G Chord

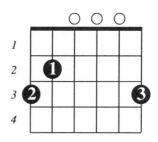

Lonesome Valley
Strum Style
Using Full G Chords

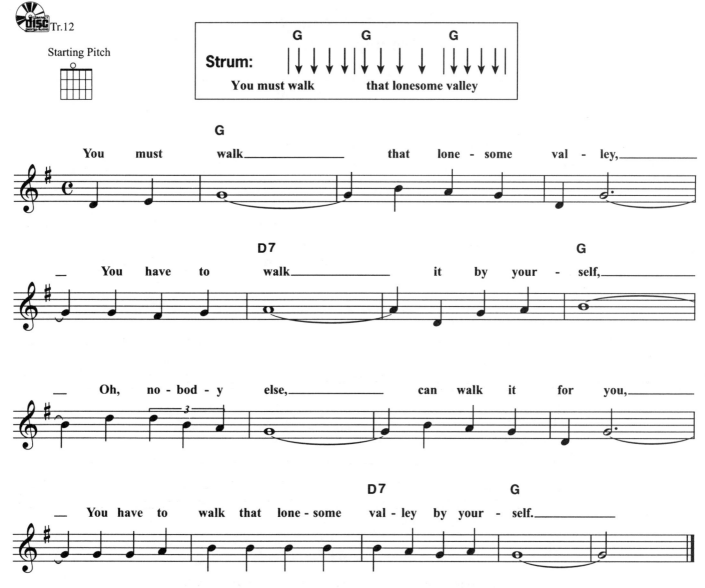

Full G Chord Arpeggio Style

With the full G chord, the thumb moves to the 6th string.

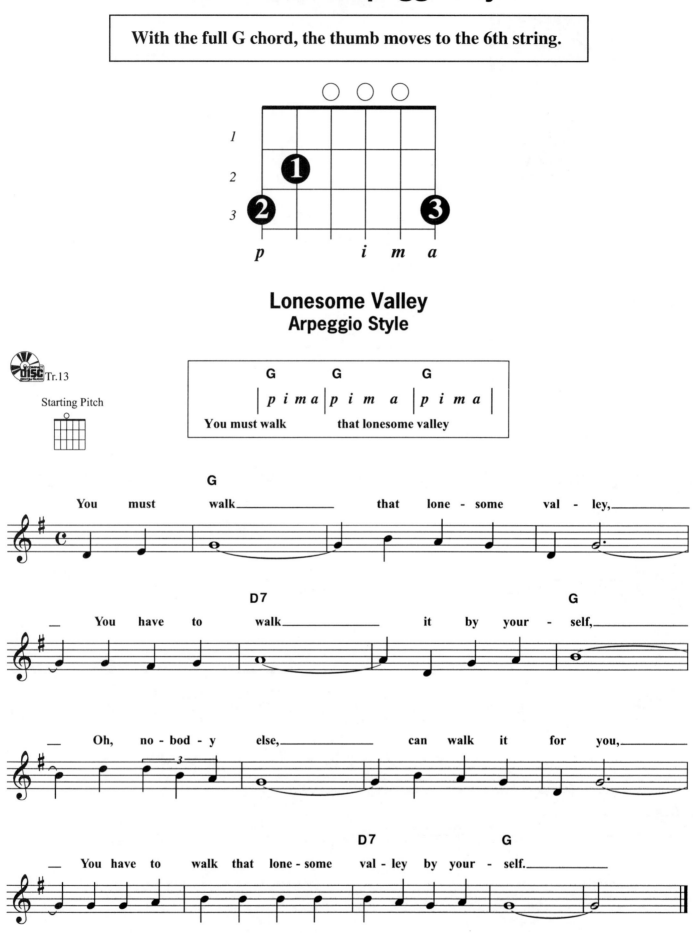

Lonesome Valley
Arpeggio Style

Lonesome Valley
Double Arpeggio Pattern

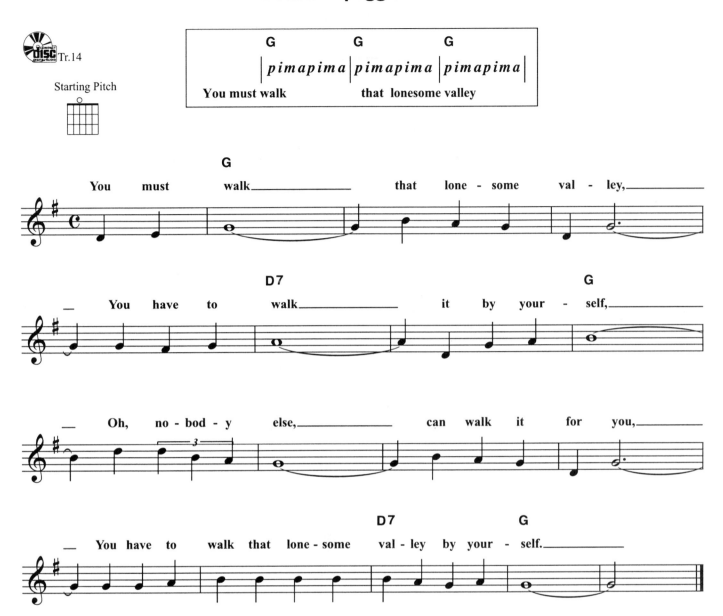

Tr.14

Starting Pitch

Alternate Bass

G Chords

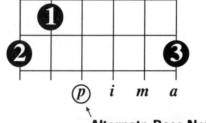

Normal Bass Note

Alternate Bass Note

D7 Chords

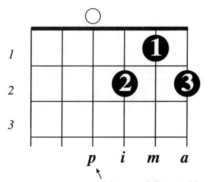

Normal Bass Note

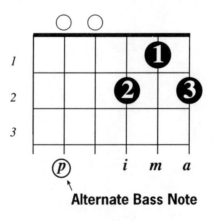

Alternate Bass Note

Alternate Bass Note Practice

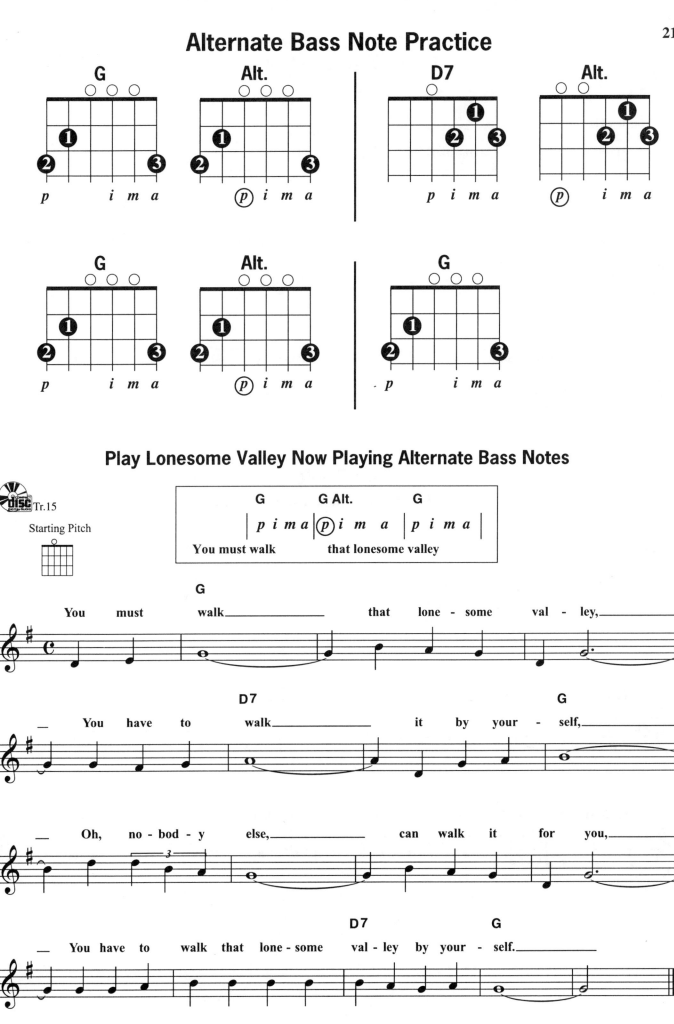

Play Lonesome Valley Now Playing Alternate Bass Notes

Tom Dooley
Double Arpeggio Pattern

Old Chisholm Trail
Double Arpeggio Pattern

Cowboy Song

Skip to my Lou
Double Arpeggio/Alternate Bass

2. Left and right oh skip to my lou.
3. Fly in the buttermilk skip to my lou.

Long Long Ago
Double Arpeggio/Alternate Bass

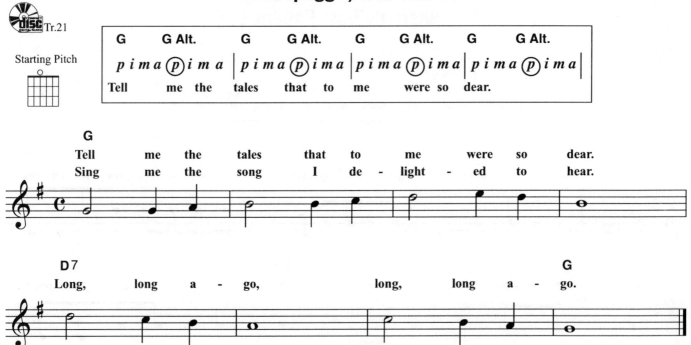

3/4 Time

In 3/4 time we have 3 beats per measure.

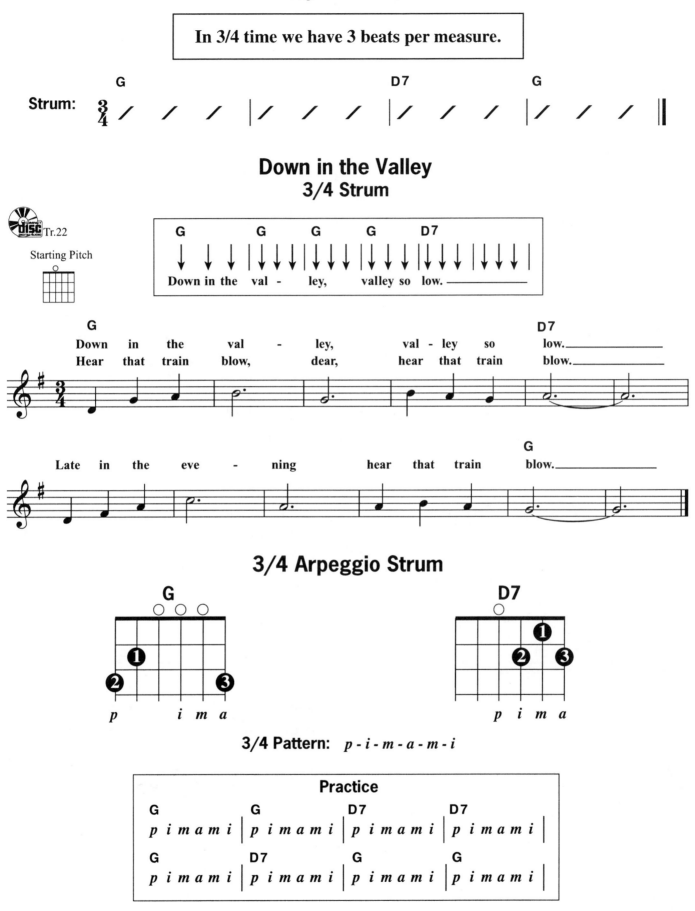

Down in the Valley
3/4 Strum

3/4 Arpeggio Strum

3/4 Pattern: *p - i - m - a - m - i*

Practice			
G	**G**	**D7**	**D7**
p i m a m i	*p i m a m i*	*p i m a m i*	*p i m a m i*
G	**D7**	**G**	**G**
p i m a m i	*p i m a m i*	*p i m a m i*	*p i m a m i*

Down in the Valley
3/4 Arpeggio Pattern

Oh, My Darling Clementine
3/4 Arpeggio Pattern

C Chord

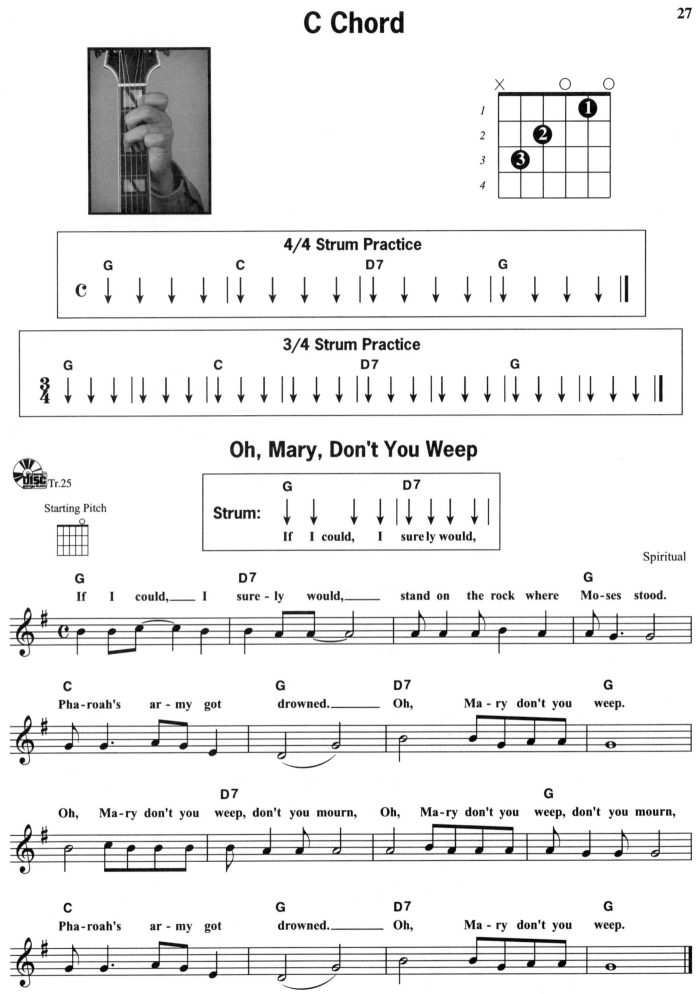

4/4 Strum Practice

G   C   D7   G

3/4 Strum Practice

G   C   D7   G

Oh, Mary, Don't You Weep

Tr.25

Starting Pitch

Strum: G   D7

If   I could,   I   surely would,

Spiritual

G   D7   G

If I could,___ I sure-ly would,___ stand on the rock where Mo-ses stood.

C   G   D7   G

Pha-roah's ar-my got drowned._____ Oh, Ma-ry don't you weep.

D7   G

Oh, Ma-ry don't you weep, don't you mourn, Oh, Ma-ry don't you weep, don't you mourn,

C   G   D7   G

Pha-roah's ar-my got drowned._____ Oh, Ma-ry don't you weep.

3/4 Strum

Blow Ye Winds, Westerly

Tr.26

Starting Pitch

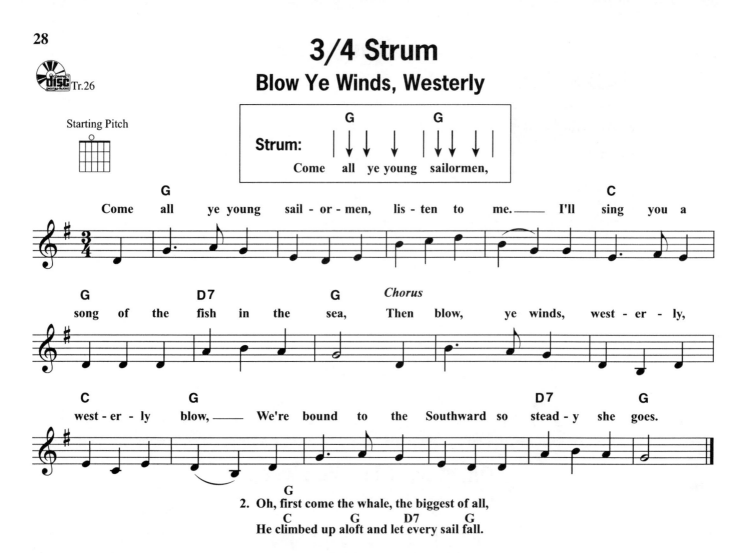

Strum:

Come all ye young sailormen,

Come all ye young sail-or-men, lis-ten to me.___ I'll sing you a
song of the fish in the sea, Then blow, ye winds, west-er-ly,
west-er-ly blow,___ We're bound to the Southward so stead-y she goes.

2. Oh, first come the whale, the biggest of all,
He climbed up aloft and let every sail fall.

Double Arpeggio Pattern Using C

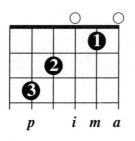

p   i   m   a

Practice			
G	C	D7	G
𝄵 p i m a p i m a	p i m a p i m a	p i m a p i m a	p i m a p i m a ‖

3/4 Arpeggio Using C

Practice			
G	C	D7	G
¾ p i m a m i	p i m a m i	p i m a m i	p i m a m i ‖

Our Team Will Shine Tonight

Jack of Diamonds

2. My foot's in the stirrup,
My bridle's in hand,
I'm leaving sweet Molly,
The fairest in the land.

3. Her parents don't like me,
They say I'm too poor,
They say I'm unworthy,
To enter her door.

C Alternate Bass

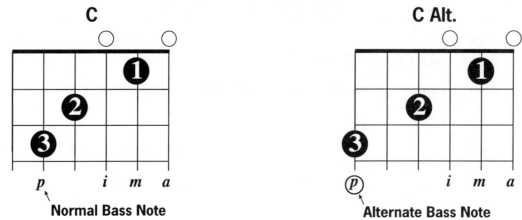

Normal Bass Note

Alternate Bass Note

She'll Be Coming 'Round the Mountain
Alternate Bass Pattern

Tr.29

Starting Pitch

2. She'll be riding six white horses when she comes.

3. And we'll all be out to meet her when she comes.

D Chord

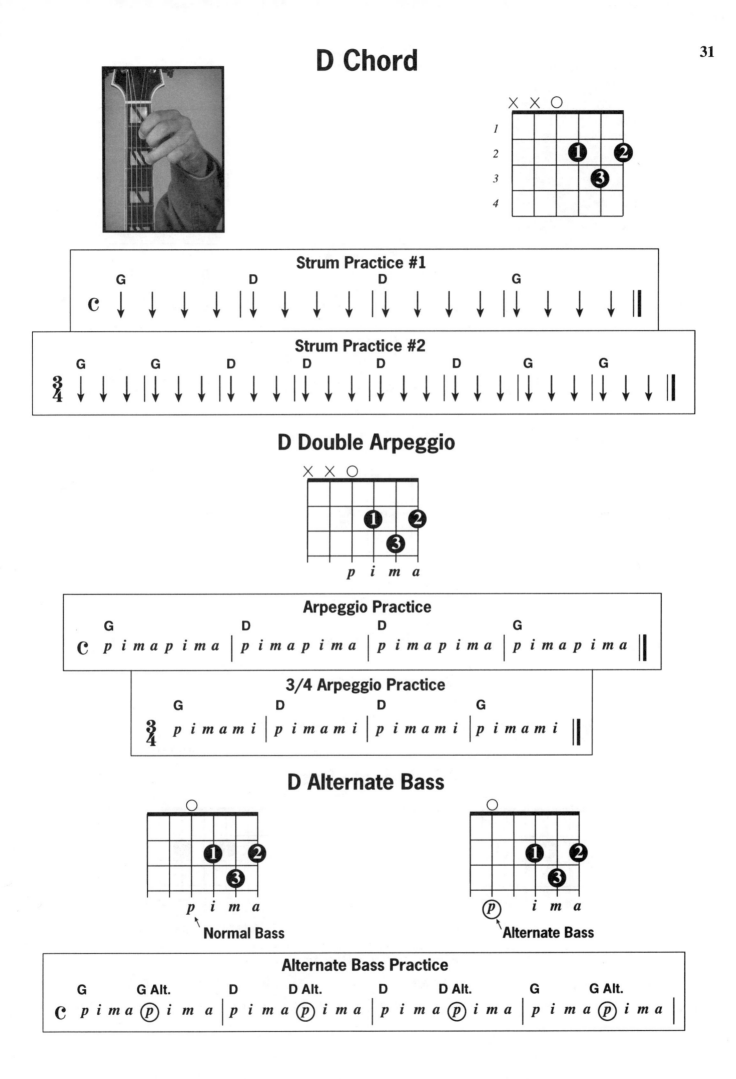

A7 Chord

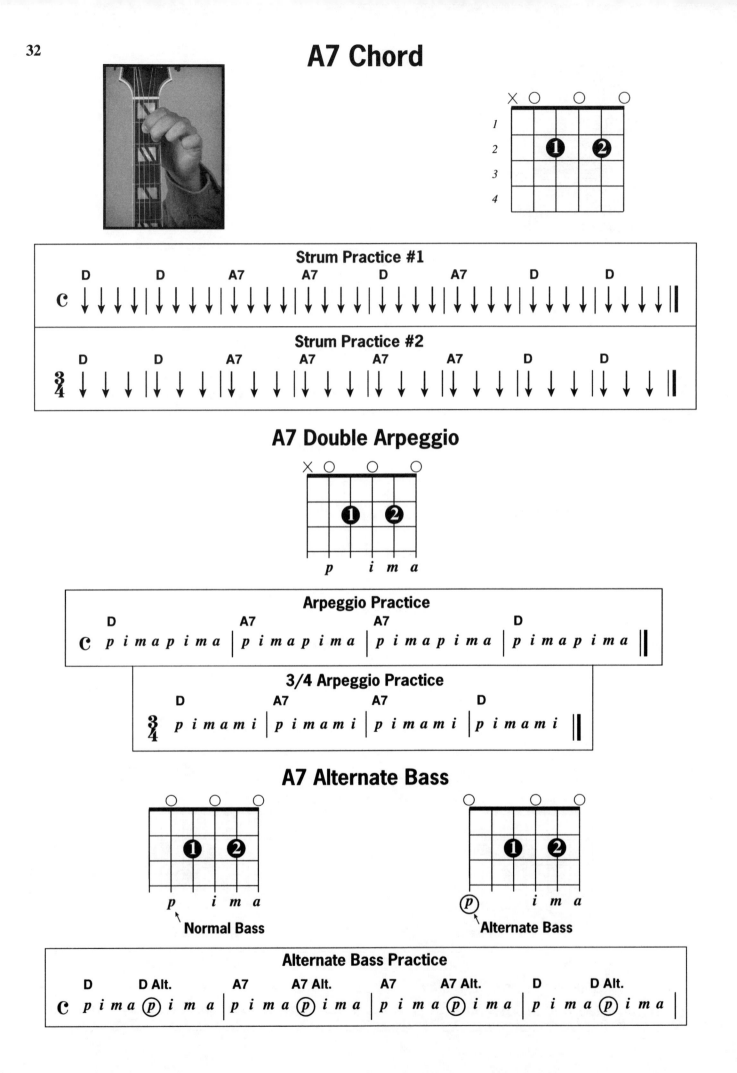

Strum Practice #1

D   D   A7   A7   D   A7   D   D

Strum Practice #2

D   D   A7   A7   A7   A7   D   D

A7 Double Arpeggio

p   i   m   a

Arpeggio Practice

D   *p i m a p i m a* | A7   *p i m a p i m a* | A7   *p i m a p i m a* | D   *p i m a p i m a*

3/4 Arpeggio Practice

D   *p i m a m i* | A7   *p i m a m i* | A7   *p i m a m i* | D   *p i m a m i*

A7 Alternate Bass

p   i   m   a
Normal Bass

(p)   i   m   a
Alternate Bass

Alternate Bass Practice

D   D Alt.   A7   A7 Alt.   A7   A7 Alt.   D   D Alt.

p i m a (p) *i m a* | *p i m a* (p) *i m a* | *p i m a* (p) *i m a* | *p i m a* (p) *i m a*

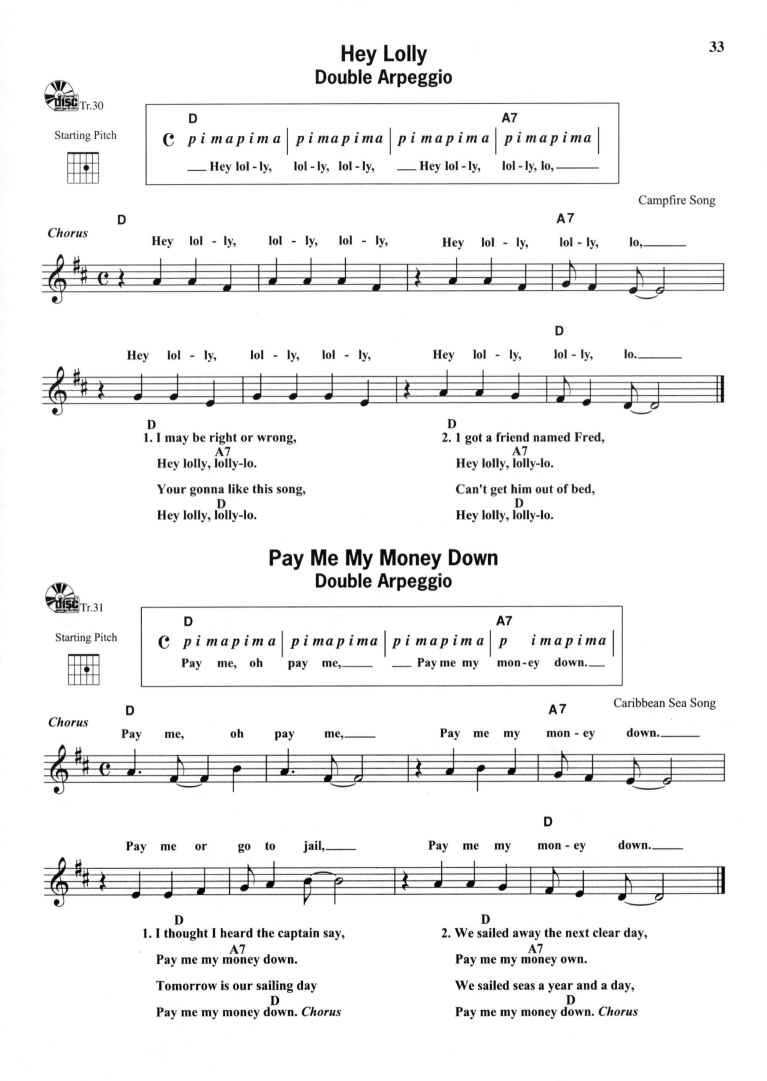

Hey Lolly
Double Arpeggio

Tr.30

Starting Pitch

D			A7
C *pimapima*	*pimapima*	*pimapima*	*pimapima*
___ Hey lol - ly,	lol - ly, lol - ly,	___ Hey lol - ly,	lol - ly, lo, ___

Campfire Song

Chorus

D
Hey lol - ly, lol - ly, lol - ly,   Hey lol - ly, lol - ly, lo, ___ (A7)

Hey lol - ly, lol - ly, lol - ly,   Hey lol - ly, lol - ly, lo. ___ (D)

D
1. I may be right or wrong,
A7
Hey lolly, lolly-lo.

Your gonna like this song,
D
Hey lolly, lolly-lo.

D
2. 1 got a friend named Fred,
A7
Hey lolly, lolly-lo.

Can't get him out of bed,
D
Hey lolly, lolly-lo.

Pay Me My Money Down
Double Arpeggio

Tr.31

Starting Pitch

D			A7
C *pimapima*	*pimapima*	*pimapima*	*p imapima*
Pay me, oh pay me, ___	___ Pay me my	mon-ey down. ___	

Caribbean Sea Song

Chorus

D
Pay me, oh pay me, ___   Pay me my mon - ey down. ___ (A7)

Pay me or go to jail, ___   Pay me my mon - ey down. ___ (D)

D
1. I thought I heard the captain say,
A7
Pay me my money down.

Tomorrow is our sailing day
D
Pay me my money down. *Chorus*

D
2. We sailed away the next clear day,
A7
Pay me my money own.

We sailed seas a year and a day,
D
Pay me my money down. *Chorus*

On Top of Old Smoky
3/4 Arpeggio

Auld Lang Syne
Alternate Bass

Another 3/4 Pattern
p i m a m a

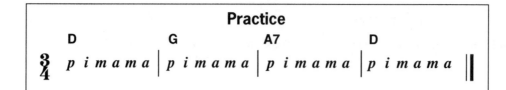

Another Pattern

Bass-Pluck-Pluck | Alt. Bass-Pluck-Pluck

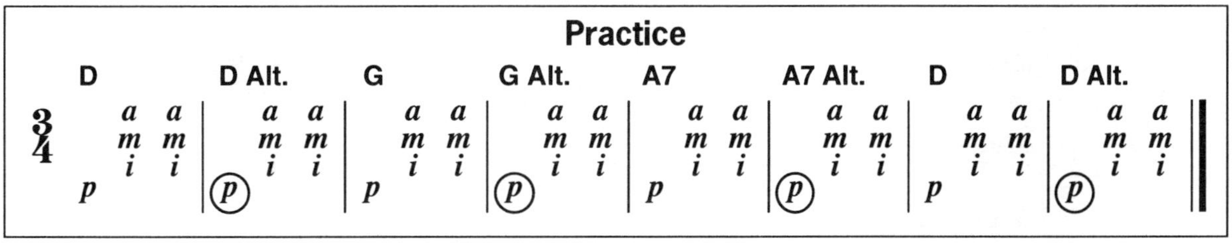

Beautiful Brown Eyes
Bass-Pluck-Pluck Pattern

Tr.35

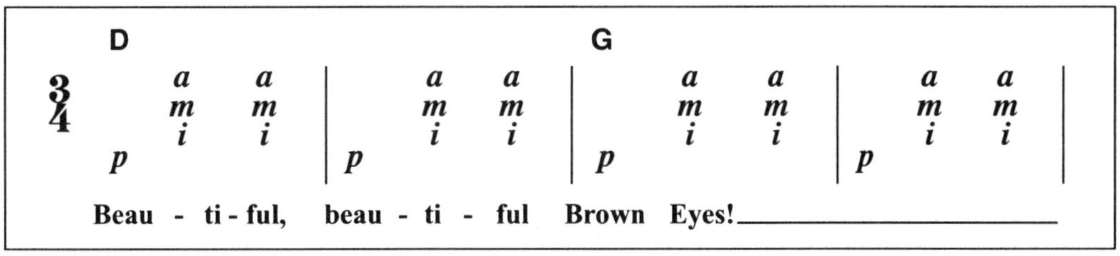

Starting Pitch

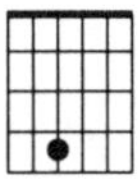

Country Waltz

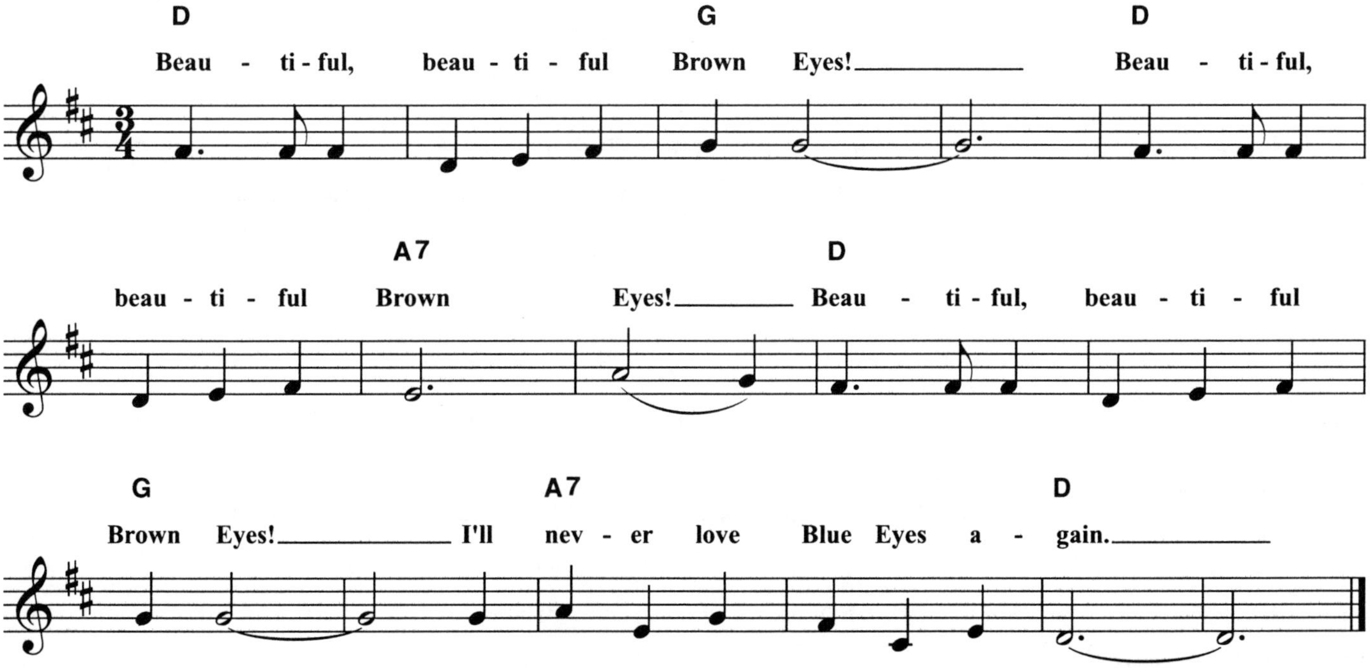

E Minor

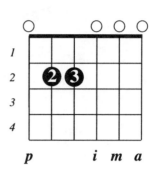

p   i m a

E Minor Strum Practice

Em   D   Em

C ↓ ↓ ↓ ↓ |↓ ↓ ↓ ↓ |↓ ↓ ↓ ↓ |↓ ↓ ↓ ↓ ‖

E Minor Arpeggio Practice

Em   D   Em

C *p i m a p i m a* | *p i m a p i m a* | *p i m a p i m a* | *p i m a p i m a* ‖

Hey, Ho, Nobody Home
Arpeggio Pattern

Tr.36

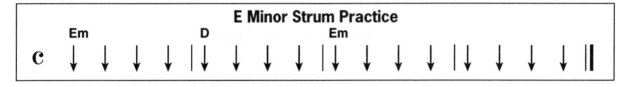

Em   D   Em   D   Em   D   Em   D

C *p i m a p i m a* | *p i m a p i m a* | *p i m a p i m a* | *p i m a p i m a* |

Hey,   ho   no - body home.   Meat, nor drink, nor   money have I none.

Starting Pitch

Em   D   Em   D   Em   D

Hey,   ho   no - bod - y   home.   Meat,   nor   drink,   nor

Em   D   Em   D   Em   D   Em

mon - ey have I none.   Still   I   will   be   mer - - - ry.

Fingerpicking Chord Reference Chart

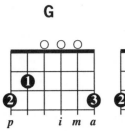
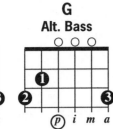
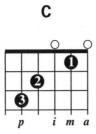
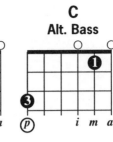
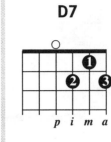
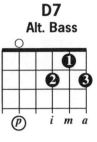

G   G Alt. Bass   C   C Alt. Bass   D7   D7 Alt. Bass

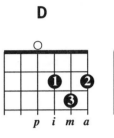
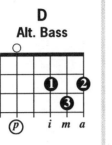
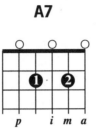
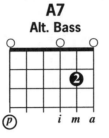
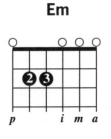
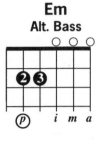

D   D Alt. Bass   A7   A7 Alt. Bass   Em   Em Alt. Bass

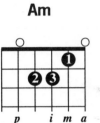
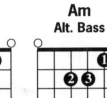
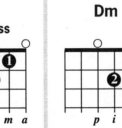
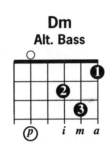
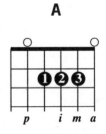

Am   Am Alt. Bass   Dm   Dm Alt. Bass   A   A Alt. Bass

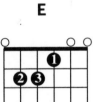
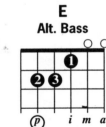
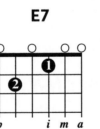
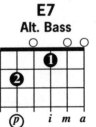
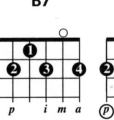

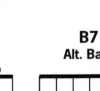

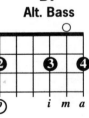

E   E Alt. Bass   E7   E7 Alt. Bass   B7   B7 Alt. Bass

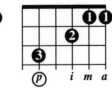

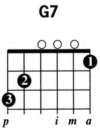
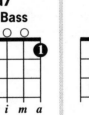
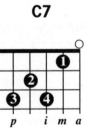
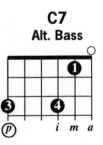

F   F Alt. Bass   G7   G7 Alt. Bass   C7   C7 Alt. Bass